# Crafts for Kids Who Are Wild About

## Polar Life

Crafts for Kids Who Are

# WILD

## ABOUT
## POLAR LIFE

By Kathy Ross
Illustrated by Sharon Lane Holm

The Millbrook Press   Brookfield, Connecticut

For Sharon, whose pictures brought this series to life—K.R.
For Kathy, whose words and projects brought inspiration—S.L.H.

Library of Congress Cataloging-in-Publication Data
Ross, Kathy (Katharine Reynolds), 1948–
Crafts for kids who are wild about polar life / Kathy Ross ; illustrated by Sharon Lane Holm.
p. cm. — (Crafts for kids who are wild about)
Includes bibliographical references.
Summary: Provides instructions for twenty projects featuring arctic animals, such as a penguin pin, harp seal puppet, walrus mask, fuzzy polar bear, and stuffed caribou.
ISBN 0-7613-0955-1 (lib. bdg.)
1. Handicraft—Juvenile literature. 2. Animals in art—Juvenile literature. 3. Animals—Polar regions—Juvenile literature. [1. Animals in art. 2. Handicraft. 3. Animals—Polar regions.] I. Holm, Sharon Lane, ill. II. Title.
III. Series: Ross, Kathy (Katharine Reynolds), 1948–    Crafts for kids who are wild about.
TT160.R7142252   1998
745.5—dc21   98-4580   CIP   AC

Published by The Millbrook Press, Inc.
2 Old New Milford Road
Brookfield, Connecticut 06804

# Contents

# Introduction

This book of crafts tells how to make some of the animals that live in the very coldest places on our earth, the polar regions. The temperature in these regions rarely goes above freezing, so the land and the surrounding seas are frozen for much of the year.

The Arctic is made up of the Arctic Ocean and the land around it, which is called the tundra. Many animals spend their summer in the Arctic, and others stay there year-round.

The Antarctic consists of the continent of Antarctica, the Southern Ocean surrounding it, and the islands in the Southern Ocean. Antarctica is so cold that only a few plants and some insects manage to survive there. However, the waters surrounding Antarctica support a variety of life forms.

I have given you project ideas for some of my favorite polar animals. I hope they will make you want to find out more about the way these creatures live and survive in the frozen world of the North and South Poles.

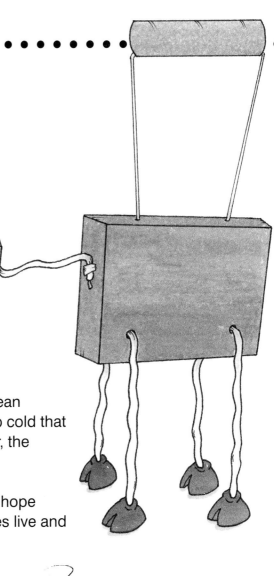

# Penguin Pin

## Here is what you need:

three wooden ice-cream spoons
black poster paint and a paintbrush
white glue
fiberfill
scrap of orange felt
two wiggle eyes
masking tape
pin backing or safety pin
Styrofoam tray for drying

Penguins are birds that cannot fly in the air, but they "fly" underwater, using the same muscles other birds use to fly in the air.

## Here is what you do:

 Paint one side and the edge of two of the ice-cream spoons black. Put them on the Styrofoam tray to dry.

 Use glue to cover one side of the third spoon with a thin layer of fiberfill.

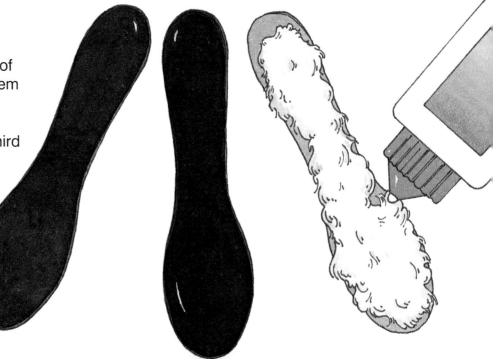

Glue the handle ends of the two black spoons together so that the bowl ends flare out on each side to make wings. Glue the fiberfill-covered spoon behind and between the wings so that the white fiberfill forms the tummy of the penguin.

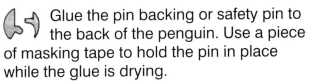

Cut a triangle-shaped beak from the orange felt scrap. Glue the two wiggle eyes and the beak on the black overlapped handles above the white tummy.

Glue the pin backing or safety pin to the back of the penguin. Use a piece of masking tape to hold the pin in place while the glue is drying.

This penguin also makes a very nice refrigerator magnet. Just use a piece of sticky-back magnet instead of the pin.

# Rockhopper Penguin

## Here is what you need:

black and orange construction paper
plastic sandwich bag
white Styrofoam packing pieces
three black craft feathers
two yellow craft feathers
two white hole reinforcers
pencil
scissors
white glue
stapler

The little rockhopper penguin does just as its name implies; it hops from rock to rock to get up and down the cliffs where it nests.

## Here is what you do:

Fill the plastic bag about three-quarters full with Styrofoam packing pieces. Fold the top of the bag over and staple it shut. This will be the white front of the penguin.

Lay the filled bag flat on the black paper. Use the pencil to draw a penguin shape around the bag. Make a head at the top of the bag, a tail at the bottom, and a wing on each side. Cut the penguin shape out.

Staple the top of the bag to the penguin shape to form the white tummy. Fold the wings forward.

Cut a triangle-shaped beak from the orange paper. Glue the flat end of the beak to the head. Stick the two hole reinforcers above the beak for eyes. Glue a yellow feather above each eye.

Bend back the tail feather at the bottom of the penguin. Staple the black craft feathers to the tail.

Cut two feet for the penguin from orange paper. Staple the top of each foot to the bottom of the penguin, then bend the feet forward.

Stand your little rockhopper on a shelf—but be careful that he doesn't hop off!

# Emperor Penguin

## Here is what you need:

oatmeal box
black construction paper
fiberfill
scissors
white glue
orange poster paint and a paintbrush
two hole reinforcers
two peppercorns
pencil

The emperor penguin has a flap of skin above the feet that is used to keep its baby warm before and after hatching.

## Here is what you do:

Cut down opposite sides of the box and then halfway around the bottom to remove one side of the box.

Cut a piece of black paper to cover the remaining outside of the box. Glue the paper in place. Continue with the next step while the glue is still wet.

Trace around the lid of the oatmeal box to get an idea of the size for the head. Draw a long triangle shape off one side of the traced circle for the beak. Cut out the head and beak. Slip the edge of the circle head behind the top edge of the box and the glued paper. Do not fold the head forward yet.

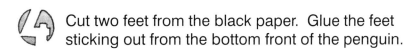

Cut two feet from the black paper. Glue the feet sticking out from the bottom front of the penguin.

Cover the inside of the box with glue. Fill in the entire box opening with fiberfill to form the tummy of the penguin.

Fold the head forward over the fiberfill front of the penguin. Crease the triangle beak in the center. Glue the head in place over the fiberfill.

Dab orange paint on each side of the head and along each side of the beak.

Stick the two hole reinforcers on the head for eyes. Glue a peppercorn in the center of each eye for a pupil.

Shape an egg from aluminum foil to tuck under the tummy of the penguin. To give the egg the light-brown color of an emperor penguin egg, cover the foil with a layer of glue and facial tissue. Let the glued tissue dry hard, then paint it light brown.

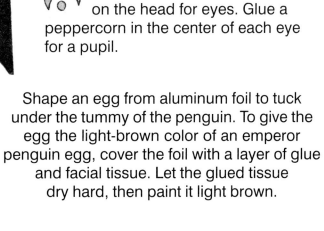

# Hands and Foot Arctic Tern

## Here is what you need:

white, black, and orange construction paper
pencil
black marker
scissors
white glue

## Here is what you do:

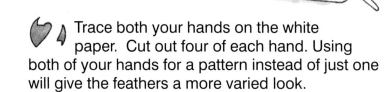

The arctic tern travels from the Arctic to the Antarctic and back again each year. This bird holds the record for the longest distance traveled in a year.

**1)** Trace around your foot on the white paper. Cut out the foot shape to use as the body for your bird.

**2)** Trace both your hands on the white paper. Cut out four of each hand. Using both of your hands for a pattern instead of just one will give the feathers a more varied look.

**3)** The heel of the foot shape will be the head of the bird. Cut out a long pointed beak from the orange paper. Glue the end of the beak on the end of the heel of the foot shape.

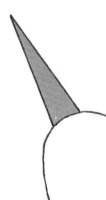

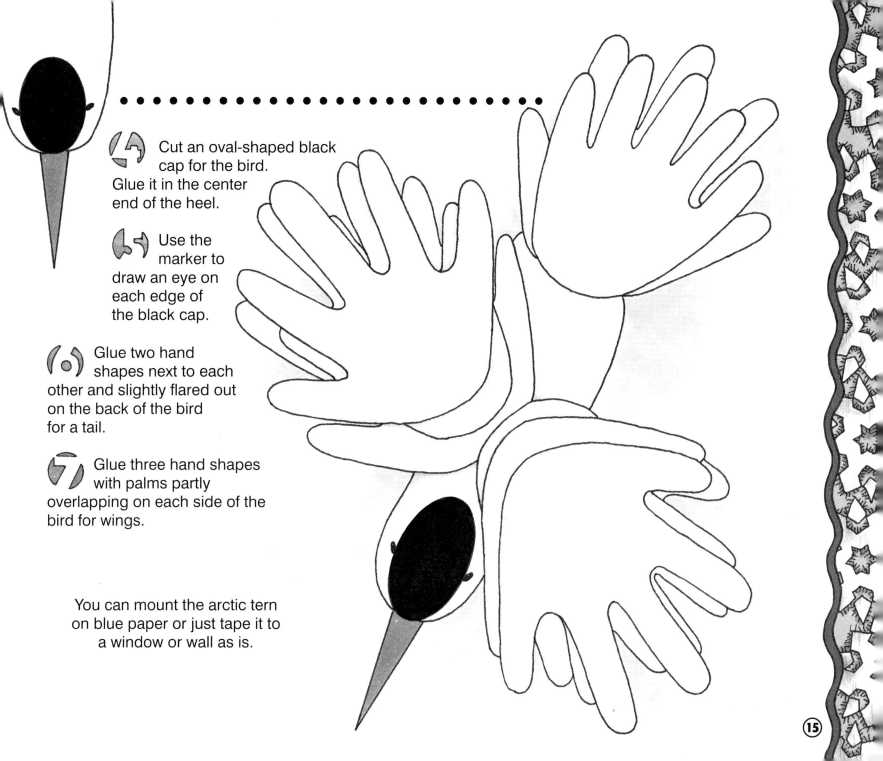

4 Cut an oval-shaped black cap for the bird. Glue it in the center end of the heel.

5 Use the marker to draw an eye on each edge of the black cap.

6 Glue two hand shapes next to each other and slightly flared out on the back of the bird for a tail.

7 Glue three hand shapes with palms partly overlapping on each side of the bird for wings.

You can mount the arctic tern on blue paper or just tape it to a window or wall as is.

# Snowy Owl Chicks Wall Hanging

## Here is what you need:

three pinecones of different sizes
fiberfill
white glue
9-inch (23-cm) paper plate
yellow and black paper scraps
blue poster paint and a paintbrush
thin ribbon or yarn
hole punch
scissors
newspaper to work on

The chicks in the nest of a snowy owl will be of different sizes and ages because the owl, unlike most other birds, incubates each egg as it is laid.

## Here is what you do:

1. To make each chick, wrap a pinecone in a thin layer of fiberfill, with the brown petals of the pinecone sticking through.

2. Cut eyes from yellow paper. Punch pupils from the black paper and glue a pupil in the center of each eye. Glue two eyes on one side of one end of the pinecone.

3. Cut triangle beaks for the owls from black paper. Glue them in place under the eyes to complete the faces of the owls.

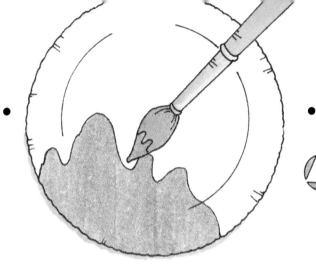

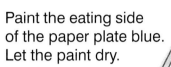 Paint the eating side of the paper plate blue. Let the paint dry.

Glue the three owl chicks next to each other on the front of the plate. Glue a little bit of fiberfill across the bottom for snow.

Punch two holes in the top of the plate. String an 8-inch (20-cm) piece of ribbon through the two holes and tie the ends together to make a hanger for the owls.

Snowy owls build nests on the ground, but these owls will be very happy on your wall.

# Harp Seal Puppet

## Here is what you need:

cardboard toilet-tissue tube
two white Styrofoam trays
fiberfill
two paper fasteners
blue plastic wrap
aluminum foil
masking tape
white glue
scissors
black permanent marker
two small wiggle eyes
two tiny wiggle eyes
black yarn
black poster paint and a paintbrush
craft stick

Harp seals are born with fluffy white coats that darken as they grow up.

## Here is what you do:

 Cut a slit up one side of the tube, stopping about an inch from the other end. Wrap the tube around itself to form a cone shape for the body of the seal. Use masking tape to hold the cone shape. Use fiberfill to close the small opening at the point of the cone. Paint the outside of the tube and the fiberfill at the tip black.

Cut a 2-inch (5-cm) piece of black yarn. Tie a knot in the middle of the yarn and fray both ends to make whiskers for the seal. Glue the whiskers to the tip of the cone. Glue two small wiggle eyes on one side of the cone.

Glue a thin layer of fiberfill on the other side for the underbelly of the seal. Glue the end of the craft stick inside the tube on the fiberfill-covered side, to give your puppet a holder.

Hold the Styrofoam trays together and trim around the edges to look like an ice floe. Tear off a square of blue plastic wrap for the water. Put the center of the wrap between the two pieces of Styrofoam. Using paper fasteners, attach the two pieces of Styrofoam together with the blue wrap between them.

Cut a hole through the Styrofoam trays and plastic wrap so the seal can come up through the ice.

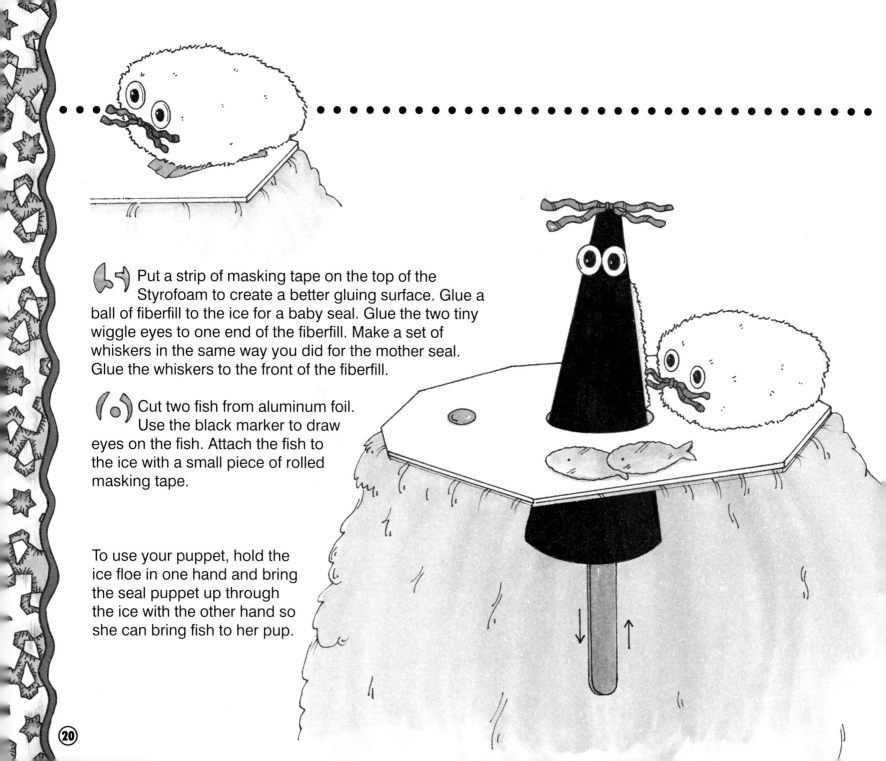

Put a strip of masking tape on the top of the Styrofoam to create a better gluing surface. Glue a ball of fiberfill to the ice for a baby seal. Glue the two tiny wiggle eyes to one end of the fiberfill. Make a set of whiskers in the same way you did for the mother seal. Glue the whiskers to the front of the fiberfill.

Cut two fish from aluminum foil. Use the black marker to draw eyes on the fish. Attach the fish to the ice with a small piece of rolled masking tape.

To use your puppet, hold the ice floe in one hand and bring the seal puppet up through the ice with the other hand so she can bring fish to her pup.

# Lemmings in a Snow Burrow

## Here is what you need:

clean tuna-fish can with label removed
fiberfill
Easter grass
four small white pom-poms
four tiny black beads
ribbon
black and orange markers
white glue
masking tape
scissors
Styrofoam tray for drying

Lemmings spend the long winter in burrows dug deep in the snow, where they dig underground trails to feeding sites.

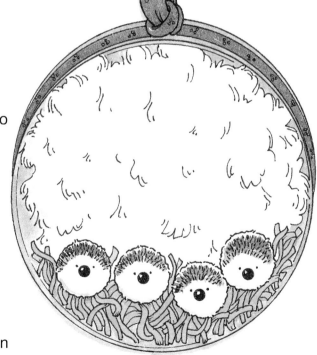

## Here is what you do:

To make each lemming, color the top and side portions of the pom-pom black and orange with the markers. Draw two black eyes at one end of the pom-pom. Glue a black bead nose below the eyes.

Put pieces of masking tape inside the can to create a better gluing surface. Turn the can on its side. Glue a thin layer of grass along the bottom of the can. Glue fiberfill over the rest of the inside of the can to look like snow.

Glue the four lemmings on the grass in the snow burrow.

Wrap the outer edge of the can with masking tape. Cover the tape with glue, then tie a piece of ribbon around the can in a knot. Tie the two ends of the ribbon together to make a hanger for the burrow.

If you would rather set your burrow on a table, you can put it on a ring of paper so that it stays upright and does not roll.

21

# Walrus Mask

## Here is what you need:

9-inch (23-cm) paper plate
brown poster paint and a paintbrush
brown construction paper
white Styrofoam tray
large black pom-pom
paper-towel tube
scissors
stapler
white glue
newspaper to work on

## Here is what you do:

1. Cut half of the inner circle out of the paper plate. The opening will be the eyehole for the mask.

2. Paint the back of the plate brown and let it dry.

3. Cut two 5-inch (13-cm) tusks from the Styrofoam tray. Staple a tusk hanging down from each side of the bottom of the mask.

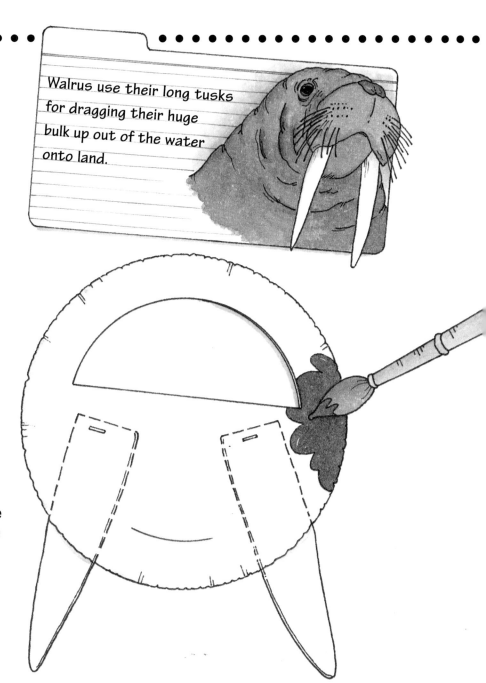

Walrus use their long tusks for dragging their huge bulk up out of the water onto land.

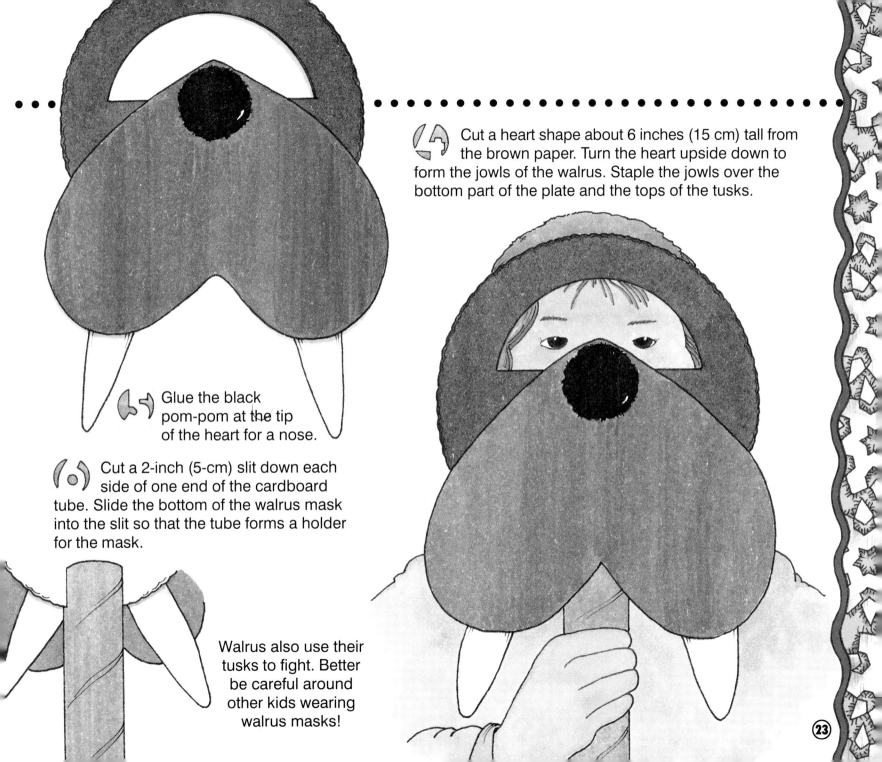

Cut a heart shape about 6 inches (15 cm) tall from the brown paper. Turn the heart upside down to form the jowls of the walrus. Staple the jowls over the bottom part of the plate and the tops of the tusks.

Glue the black pom-pom at the tip of the heart for a nose.

Cut a 2-inch (5-cm) slit down each side of one end of the cardboard tube. Slide the bottom of the walrus mask into the slit so that the tube forms a holder for the mask.

Walrus also use their tusks to fight. Better be careful around other kids wearing walrus masks!

# Fuzzy Polar Bear

## Here is what you need:

four clamp clothespins
two wooden tongue depressors
fiberfill
white felt scrap
three tiny black beads or peppercorns
small white pom-pom
scissors
white glue
Styrofoam tray for drying

The world's largest bear, the polar bear, lives in the Arctic.

## Here is what you do:

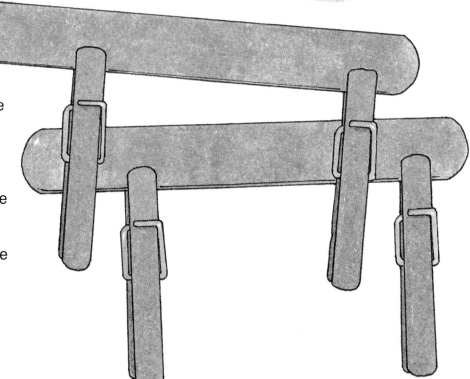

Clamp a clothespin to one end of one of the tongue depressors. Clamp a second clothespin about 1 inch (2.5 cm) from the other end of the stick. Use glue to hold the clothespins in place. Do the same thing with the second tongue depressor. The sticks will form the two sides of the body of the bear, and the clothespins will form the legs, with the head of the bear formed by the inch of stick left at one end.

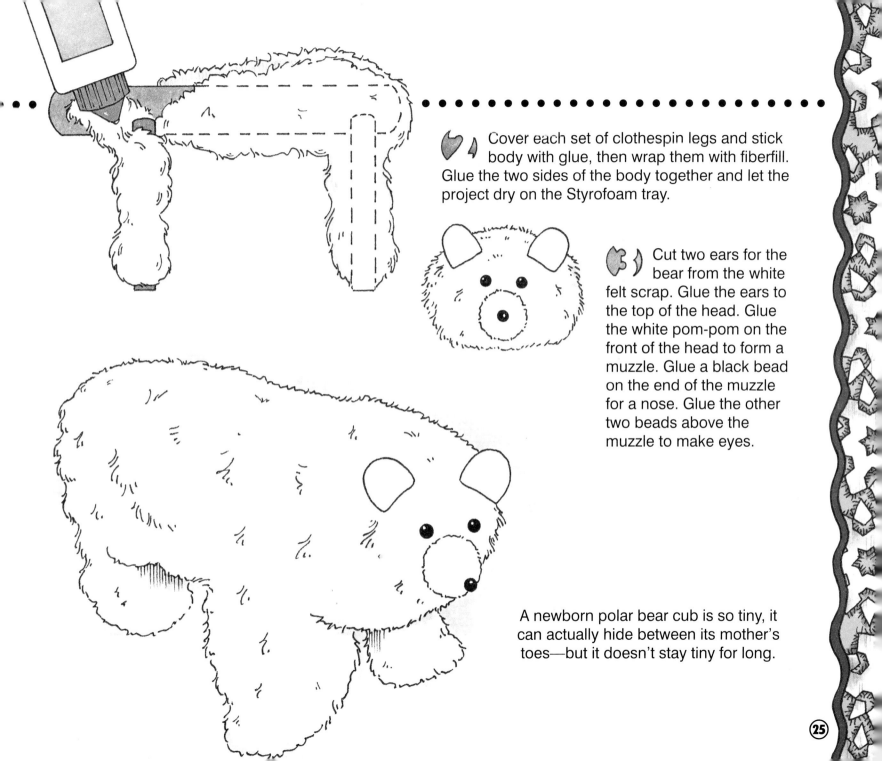

Cover each set of clothespin legs and stick body with glue, then wrap them with fiberfill. Glue the two sides of the body together and let the project dry on the Styrofoam tray.

Cut two ears for the bear from the white felt scrap. Glue the ears to the top of the head. Glue the white pom-pom on the front of the head to form a muzzle. Glue a black bead on the end of the muzzle for a nose. Glue the other two beads above the muzzle to make eyes.

A newborn polar bear cub is so tiny, it can actually hide between its mother's toes—but it doesn't stay tiny for long.

# Snarling Wolf Face

## Here is what you need:

two 9-inch (23-cm) paper plates
white Styrofoam cup
two paper fasteners
small red sock
white and black construction-paper scraps
fiberfill
gray poster paint and a paintbrush
scissors
white glue
masking tape
stapler

Arctic wolves live and hunt together in groups called packs.

## Here is what you do:

Cut the Styrofoam cup in half from top to bottom. Cut pointy teeth along the cut edges of both halves of the cup.

Overlap the rim of the two halves of the cup and hold them together with a paper fastener on each side. The two halves of the cup should now form a mouth with teeth that opens and shuts.

Hold the two plates together and, toward one edge, cut a hole in them large enough to slip the mouth through, but not large enough for the rim of the cup to go through. Put the mouth through from the eating side of one plate so that it comes out from the bottom of the plate. Use masking tape to tape the mouth to the plate. Glue the second plate over the first plate.

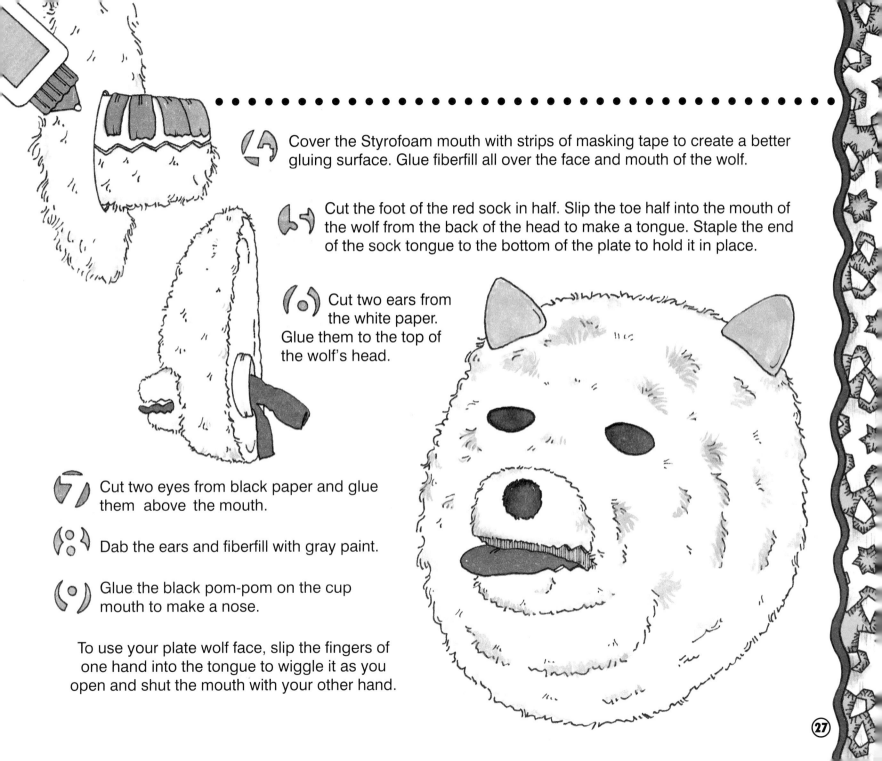

Cover the Styrofoam mouth with strips of masking tape to create a better gluing surface. Glue fiberfill all over the face and mouth of the wolf.

Cut the foot of the red sock in half. Slip the toe half into the mouth of the wolf from the back of the head to make a tongue. Staple the end of the sock tongue to the bottom of the plate to hold it in place.

Cut two ears from the white paper. Glue them to the top of the wolf's head.

Cut two eyes from black paper and glue them above the mouth.

Dab the ears and fiberfill with gray paint.

Glue the black pom-pom on the cup mouth to make a nose.

To use your plate wolf face, slip the fingers of one hand into the tongue to wiggle it as you open and shut the mouth with your other hand.

27

# Herd of Musk Oxen

## Here is what you need:

large and small spools
masking tape
pencil
brown yarn
brown and white poster board
brown poster paint and a paintbrush
white fiberfill
black marker
scissors
white glue
Styrofoam tray for drying

The shaggy musk oxen are a relative of the goat.

## Here is what you do:

You will need a spool body for each musk ox in your herd. The large spools will be the adult musk oxen, and the small spools will be the baby musk oxen. If any of the spools are plastic instead of wood, you will need to wrap the spools with masking tape to create a better gluing surface.

Use the pencil to trace around the spool on the brown poster board. Draw two legs on one side of the traced circle. Cut the circle and legs out. Trace around it and cut out a second set. Glue the legs to each end of the spool.

Draw a head on the white poster board and cut it out. Glue the head to one end of the spool. Cut two ears from the brown poster board and glue them to the top of the head. Cut long horns from the white poster board and glue them across the top of the head. Use the black marker to draw two eyes for each musk ox. Color black hooves on the end of each leg.

Cut strands of yarn long enough to hang over the spool body of the musk ox and touch the ground on both sides. Mix a small amount of white glue with brown poster paint. Cover the entire body with the paint and glue mixture, then strands of yarn.

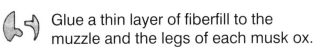

Glue a thin layer of fiberfill to the muzzle and the legs of each musk ox.

When a herd of musk oxen are attacked by wolves, the adults stand together with horns facing the attackers, ready to defend the young oxen hiding behind them.

# Mother Ringed Seal and Pup

## Here is what you need:

adult-size gray sock
child-size white sock
16-ounce (473-ml) plastic soda bottle
six small black pom-poms
fiberfill
white glue
scissors
old large marker top or lipstick tube top
white poster paint
Styrofoam tray

The mother ringed seal carves one or more dens in the snow over cracks in the ice, to keep her pup in for its first weeks of life. The extra dens allow her a place to move the pup in case of danger.

## Here is what you do:

To make the mother seal, slip the bottle, spout end first, into the foot of the sock. Cut the cuff end of the sock into a tail for the seal. Glue the sock shut. Use the scraps cut from the cuff to cut a fin for each side of the seal. Attach the fins with glue.

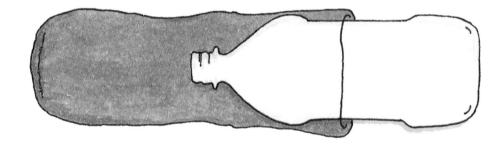

Pour some white paint into the Styrofoam tray. Use the open end of the marker top to print a pattern of white rings over the body of the seal.

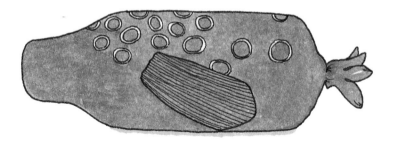

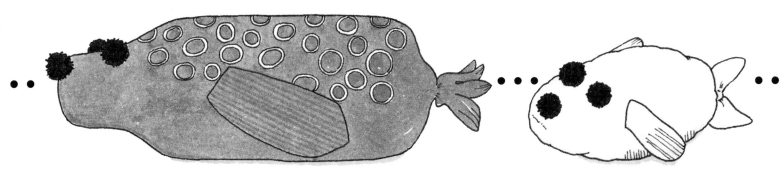

Glue a black pom-pom nose to the sock where the bottle top forms a nose for the seal. Glue two black pom-pom eyes on the head of the seal.

To make the seal pup, stuff the foot of the white sock with fiberfill. Trim the cuff into a tail. Glue the two sides of the cuff tail together to close the end of the seal. Cut fins from the cuff scraps. Glue a fin on each side of the seal.

Glue one black pom-pom to the toe of the sock to make a nose for the seal. Glue two more black pom-poms above the nose for eyes.

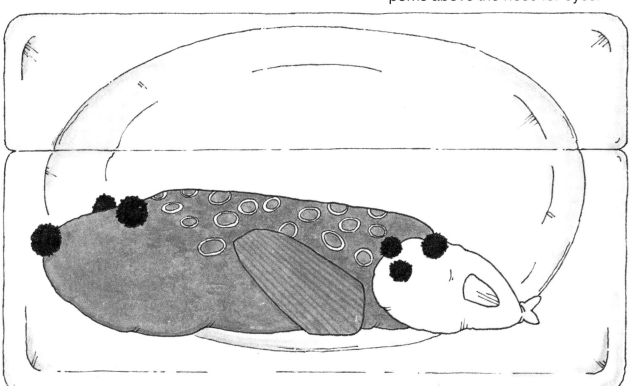

If you want to make an ice den for your seals, find some large pieces of packing Styrofoam and join them together with toothpicks.

# Changing Coat Hare

## Here is what you need:

9-inch (23-cm) paper plates
fiberfill
white, black, and brown construction paper
two clamp clothespins
brown poster paint and a paintbrush
black marker
white glue
scissors
newspaper to work on

The snowshoe hare changes from a white winter coat that hides it in the snow to a brown coat that matches the background of the short Arctic summer.

## Here is what you do:

Paint one side of the plate brown. Cover the other side of the plate with fiberfill.

To make the winter hare, fold the plate in half with the white fiberfill on the outside. Use one of the clothespins to hold the plate edges together. Cut two eyes from the black paper and glue them on each side of one end of the plate.

Position the holding clothespin just behind and above the eyes for ears. Cut two ears from the white paper. Color the tip of each ear black. Glue an ear over each side of the clothespin.

To make the summer hare, remove the white ears and fold the plate so that the brown side is on the outside. Hold the fold with the second clothespin. Cut two eyes from black paper and glue them in place. Position the clothespin above and behind the eyes for the ears. Cut two ears from brown paper. Color the tip of each ear black. Glue an ear on each side of the clothespin.

To change the coat of your snowshoe hare, just fold the plate with the desired coat on the outside and hold the fold in place with the correct color ears.

# Summer Coat and Winter Coat Stoat

## Here is what you need:

a white sock and a brown sock
two 9-inch (23-cm) paper plates
black marker
fiberfill
white glue
brown poster paint and a paintbrush
bits of yarn in shades of green and brown
stapler

The beautiful white winter coat of the stoat is called ermine.

## Here is what you do:

Turn the brown sock inside-out and put the white sock over the brown sock.

Cut off all but about 4 inches (10 cm) of the cuffs of the two socks. Cut a slit down each side of the cuff of the two socks.

Hold the two plates together, one on top of the other, and cut a hole in the center big enough for you to get your hand through. Put the cuff end of the socks in the hole of one of the plates, then staple the two sides of the cuff to the plate. Staple the second plate over the cuff side of the plate to cover the cuffs.

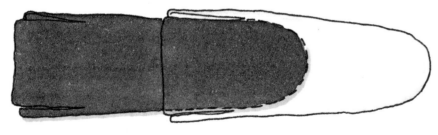

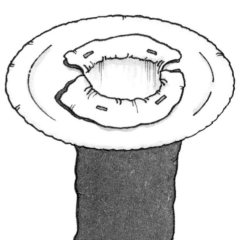

The white sock should be sticking up from one side of the plates. This will be the body of the stoat in winter. Use the black marker to draw on facial features and front legs. Glue fiberfill on the plate around the white stoat to look like snow.

Turn the sock inside-out through the hole in the plate so that the brown stoat is sticking up on the opposite side of the plates. Use the marker to draw the facial features and front legs on the brown stoat. Paint the area around the brown stoat a light brown and glue on bits of green and brown yarn for the brownish grass of the short Arctic summer.

To change your stoat from one season to the next, just turn the sock to the appropriate side. Put your hand into the sock body to make the stoat take a look around.

# Arctic Fox Cup Puppet

## Here is what you need:

two Styrofoam cups
white construction paper scrap
fiberfill
masking tape
white glue
paper fastener
two wiggle eyes
black pom-pom

The arctic fox also has the protective coloration of a changing coat.

## Here is what you do:

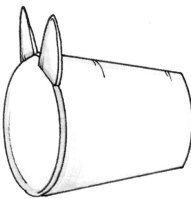 Cut two triangle-shaped ears in the rim of one cup. Trim away the rest of the rim. Turn the cup on its side for the head of the fox. Bend the ears so that they stick up at the top of the head.

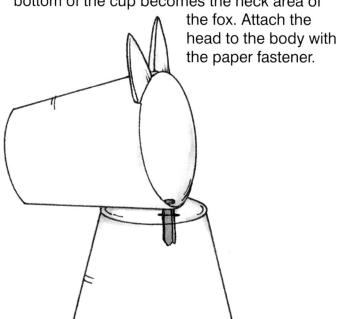 The second cup will be the body cup. Turn the cup upside-down so that the bottom of the cup becomes the neck area of the fox. Attach the head to the body with the paper fastener.

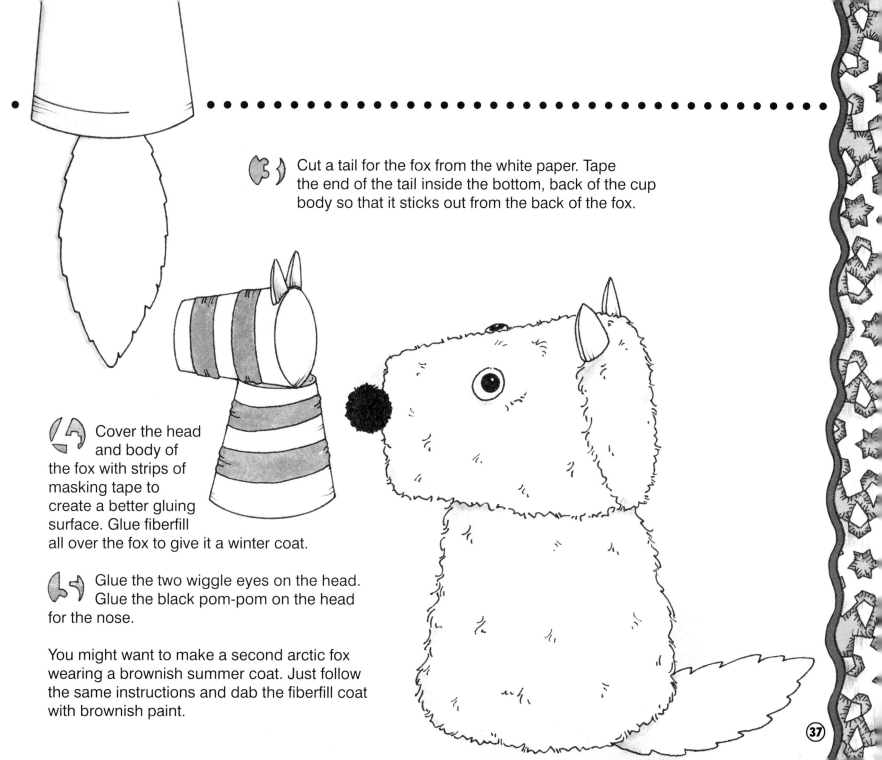

Cut a tail for the fox from the white paper. Tape the end of the tail inside the bottom, back of the cup body so that it sticks out from the back of the fox.

Cover the head and body of the fox with strips of masking tape to create a better gluing surface. Glue fiberfill all over the fox to give it a winter coat.

Glue the two wiggle eyes on the head. Glue the black pom-pom on the head for the nose.

You might want to make a second arctic fox wearing a brownish summer coat. Just follow the same instructions and dab the fiberfill coat with brownish paint.

# Stuffed Caribou

## Here is what you need:

old knit glove
brown poster paint and a paintbrush
12-inch (30-cm) brown pipe cleaner
fiberfill
brown felt scrap
two wiggle eyes
masking tape
white glue
scissors
clamp clothespins
Styrofoam tray to work on and for drying

Caribou are also called reindeer.

## Here is what you do:

Cut the brown pipe cleaner in half. Thread one piece through the glove at the base of the thumb to form the two antlers for the reindeer. Cut two pieces from the remaining pipe cleaner to wrap around each antler to make the branches of the antlers.

Lightly stuff the knit glove with fiberfill. Fold the top cuff in and glue it shut. Use the clamp clothespin to hold the two sides of the cuff together while the glue dries.

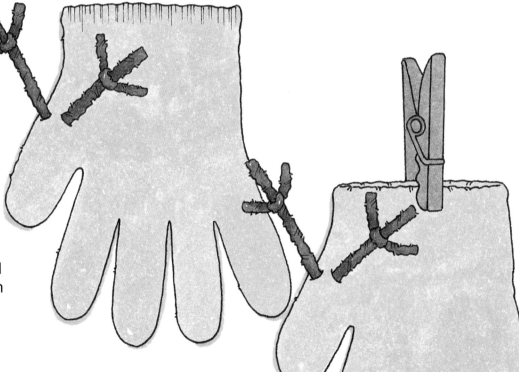

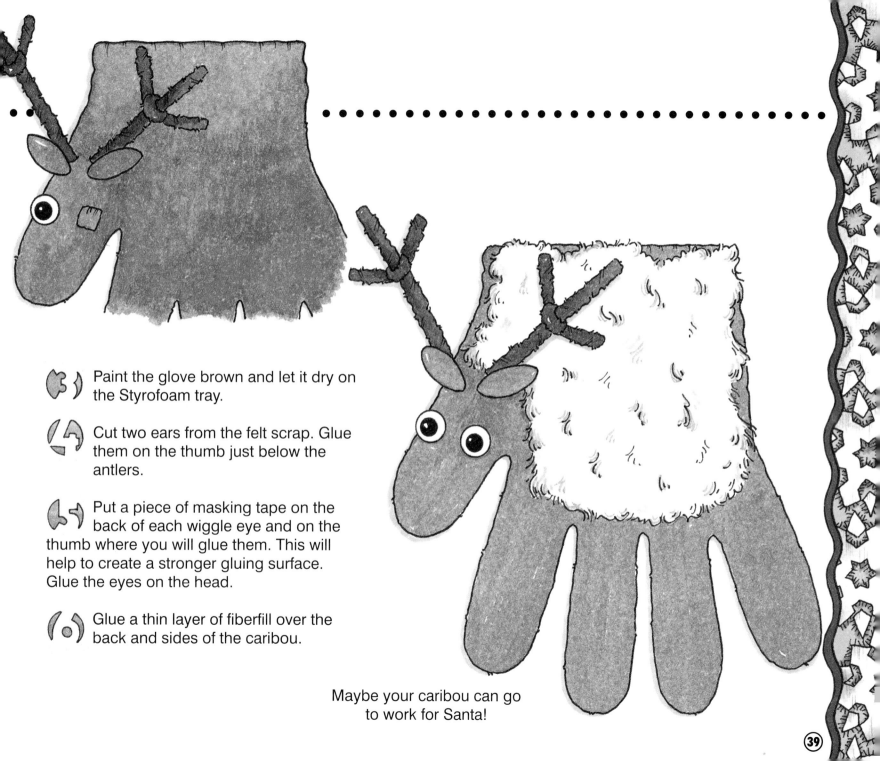

Paint the glove brown and let it dry on the Styrofoam tray.

Cut two ears from the felt scrap. Glue them on the thumb just below the antlers.

Put a piece of masking tape on the back of each wiggle eye and on the thumb where you will glue them. This will help to create a stronger gluing surface. Glue the eyes on the head.

Glue a thin layer of fiberfill over the back and sides of the caribou.

Maybe your caribou can go to work for Santa!

# Caribou Marionette

## Here is what you need:

large cereal box and a smaller food box
cardboard egg carton
black paint and a paintbrush
thick string or white shoelaces
regular string
two 12-inch (30-cm) brown pipe cleaners
brown grocery bag
black marker
clear packing tape
scissors
cardboard paper-towel tube
cardboard toilet-tissue tube

The wide hooves of the caribou act like snowshoes, making it easier for them to walk on snow.

## Here is what you do:

Cut down the seam and around the bottom of the brown grocery bag to get a flat sheet of brown paper.

Use packing tape and the brown paper to cover the boxes by wrapping them as you would a present. Leave open the paper at the open end of the two boxes.

Cut four separate egg cups from the egg carton. Cut a V-shaped notch in each one to look like the hoof of a caribou. Paint each hoof black.

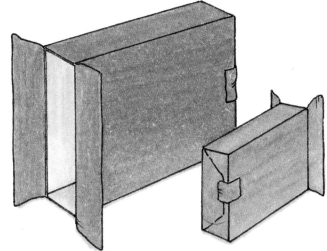

You will need two 24-inch (60-cm) shoelaces or pieces of heavy string for the legs. Turn the box on its side for the body of the caribou. Poke a hole on opposite sides of the bottom edge toward the front of the box. Make another set of holes toward the back of the box. Thread one of the strings through each set of holes so that the ends hang down on each side of the body for legs. Poke a hole in the top of each hoof. String one hoof on the end of each leg. Slide them up to the height that you want them, then knot the end of the string to hold the hoof in place. Trim off the excess string from the bottom.

Poke two holes in the top of the body. Cut a 6-foot (2-meter) piece of regular string. Thread the string down one hole and up and out the second hole. Thread one end through the paper-towel tube and tie the two ends together. The tube will be one of the holders for the marionette.

Close the open end of the box and tape the paper closed over it.

Turn the small box on its side for the head of the caribou.

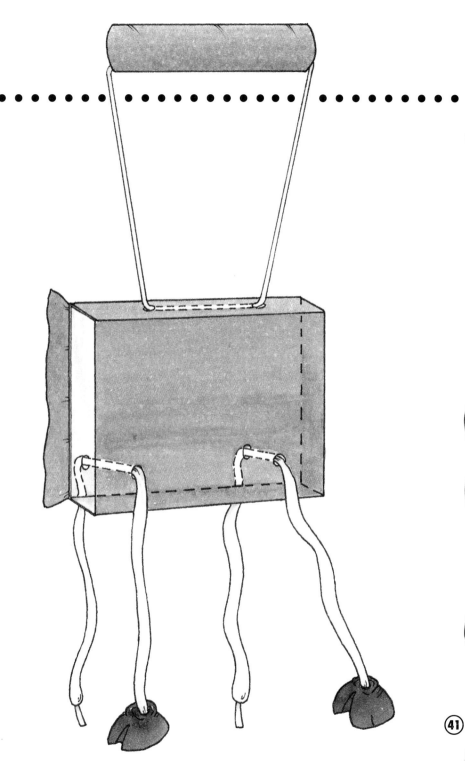

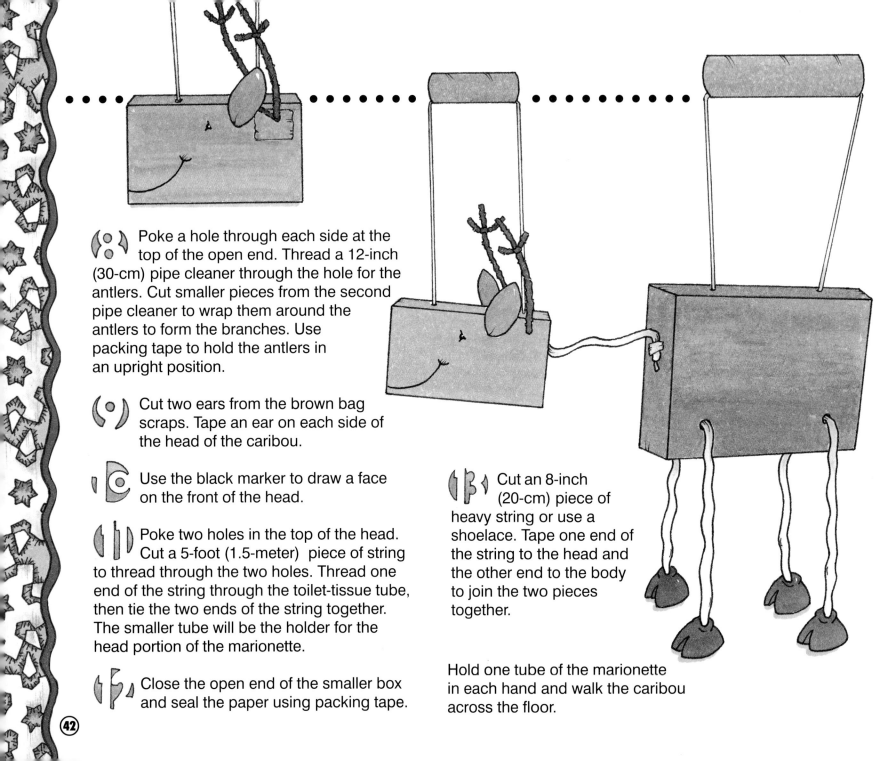

Poke a hole through each side at the top of the open end. Thread a 12-inch (30-cm) pipe cleaner through the hole for the antlers. Cut smaller pieces from the second pipe cleaner to wrap them around the antlers to form the branches. Use packing tape to hold the antlers in an upright position.

Cut two ears from the brown bag scraps. Tape an ear on each side of the head of the caribou.

Use the black marker to draw a face on the front of the head.

Poke two holes in the top of the head. Cut a 5-foot (1.5-meter) piece of string to thread through the two holes. Thread one end of the string through the toilet-tissue tube, then tie the two ends of the string together. The smaller tube will be the holder for the head portion of the marionette.

Close the open end of the smaller box and seal the paper using packing tape.

Cut an 8-inch (20-cm) piece of heavy string or use a shoelace. Tape one end of the string to the head and the other end to the body to join the two pieces together.

Hold one tube of the marionette in each hand and walk the caribou across the floor.

# Bottled Auroras

## Here is what you need:

corn syrup
package of star-shaped sequins
blue or green food coloring
16-ounce (473 ml) plastic soda bottle with a
   twist-on cap

## Here is what you do:

 Wash out the plastic bottle and remove the label.

 Pour about ½ to one cup of corn syrup into the bottle.

 Color the corn syrup with about three drops of food coloring.

 Drop 10 or more stars into the bottle.

 Put the cap back on the bottle and make sure it is tight.

Tip the bottle back and forth to evenly color the corn syrup, then tip the bottle upside-down, then right-side-up to see the colors streak through the sky.

Colorful lights, called auroras, appear in the skies of the polar regions.

If you don't have star-shaped sequins, you can make your own stars by punching them out of aluminum foil using a star-shaped punch.

# Bag Narwhal

## Here is what you need:

four large brown grocery bags
long cardboard gift-wrap tube
masking tape
black and white poster paint and a paintbrush
newspaper for stuffing and to work on
white glue
scissors
stapler
paper towels

Male and some female narwhals have a long spiral tusk growing from the upper lip.

## Here is what you do:

 Stuff the first bag almost to the top with crumpled newspaper. Stuff a second bag about three-quarters full of crumpled newspaper. Slide the bottom of the second bag into the open end of the first bag. Rub glue between the sides of the two bags where they touch to hold them together.

Stuff the bottom quarter of the third bag. Flatten the bag and cut the top three quarters into the shape of a whale tail. Staple the bag shut. Slide the bottom of the bag into the open second bag of the whale so that the tail hangs out at the end. Rub glue between the two bags to hold the tail in place.

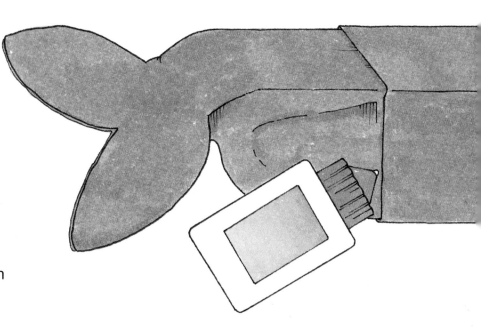

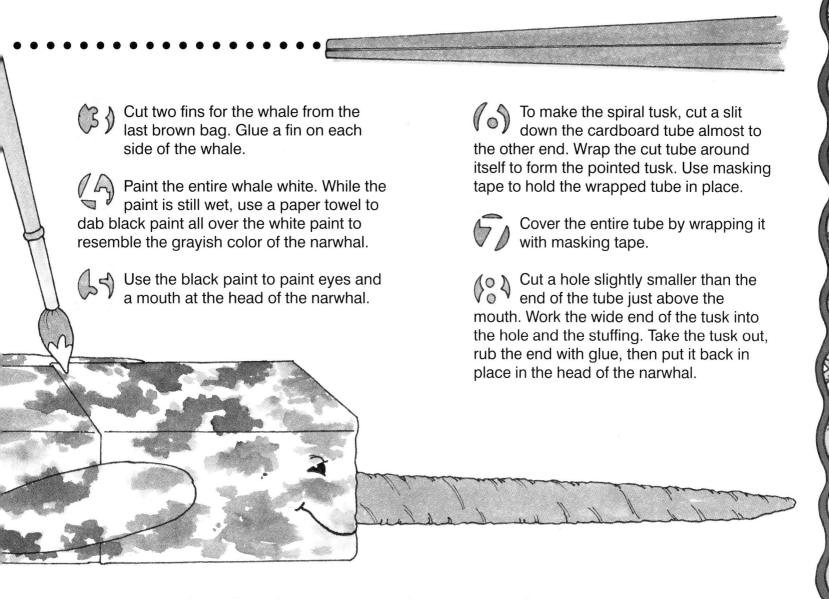

**3.** Cut two fins for the whale from the last brown bag. Glue a fin on each side of the whale.

**4.** Paint the entire whale white. While the paint is still wet, use a paper towel to dab black paint all over the white paint to resemble the grayish color of the narwhal.

**5.** Use the black paint to paint eyes and a mouth at the head of the narwhal.

**6.** To make the spiral tusk, cut a slit down the cardboard tube almost to the other end. Wrap the cut tube around itself to form the pointed tusk. Use masking tape to hold the wrapped tube in place.

**7.** Cover the entire tube by wrapping it with masking tape.

**8.** Cut a hole slightly smaller than the end of the tube just above the mouth. Work the wide end of the tusk into the hole and the stuffing. Take the tusk out, rub the end with glue, then put it back in place in the head of the narwhal.

You will need a large space to display this magnificent creature.

# Molting Beluga

## Here is what you need:

two white socks
fiberfill
scissors
white glue
black marker
two clamp clothespins

The beluga whale molts, and is thought to rub the old skin off on the ocean floor.

## Here is what you do:

1. Stuff the foot of one white sock with fiberfill. Cut the cuff of the sock into a tail for the whale. Glue the top and bottom side of the tail together. Use clamp clothespins to hold the sock shut until the glue dries.

2. Cut two fins from the sock cuff scraps. Glue one on each side of the whale.

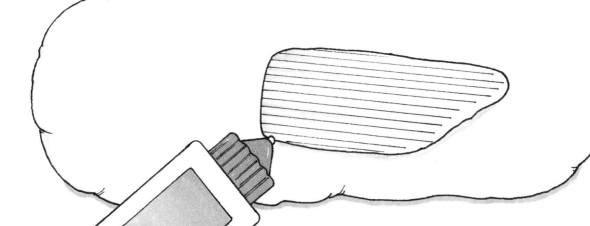

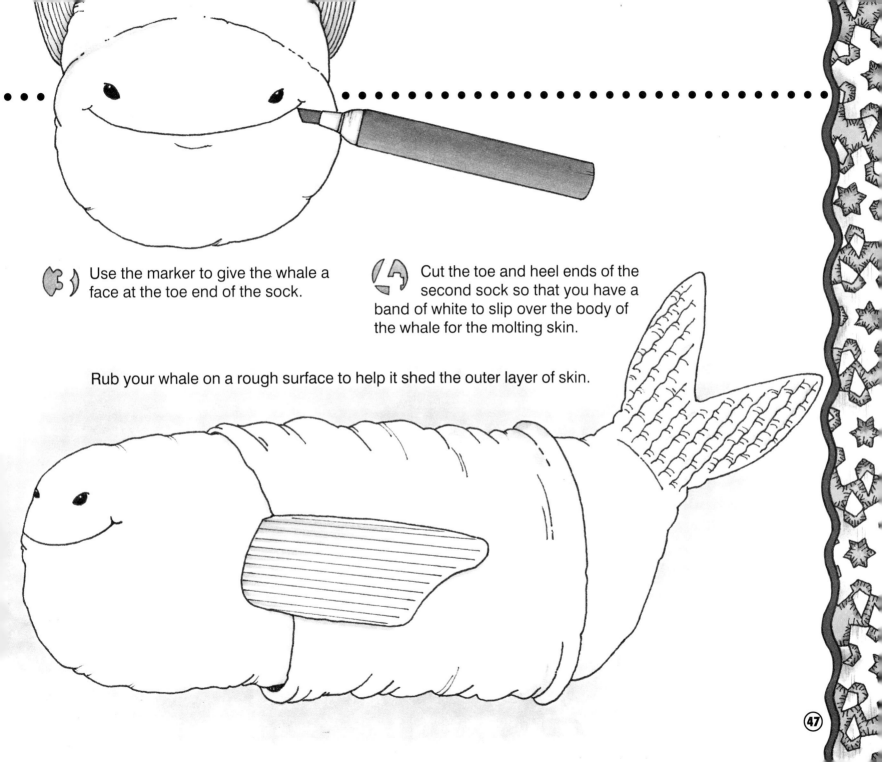

Use the marker to give the whale a face at the toe end of the sock.

Cut the toe and heel ends of the second sock so that you have a band of white to slip over the body of the whale for the molting skin.

Rub your whale on a rough surface to help it shed the outer layer of skin.

# Books About Polar Life

Barrett, Norman S. *Polar Animals.* London: Franklin Watts, 1988.

Bender, Lionel. *Polar Animals.* New York: Gloucester Press, 1989.

Chinery, Michael. *Questions and Answers About Polar Animals.* New York: Kingfisher Books, 1994.

Gilbreath, Alice Thompson. *The Arctic and Antarctica: Roof and Floor of the World.* Minneapolis: Dillon Press, 1988.

Huntington, Lee Pennock. *The Arctic and Antarctic: What Lives There.* New York: Coward, McCann and Geoghegan, 1975.

Johnson, Sylvia A. *Animals of the Polar Regions.* Minneapolis: Lerner Publications Co., 1976.

Khanduri, Kamini. *Polar Wildlife.* London: Usborne Publishing, 1992.

Lambert, David. *Polar Regions.* Morristown, NJ: Silver Burdett Press, 1988.

Pearce, Q.L. *Killer Whales and Other Frozen World Wonders.* Englewood Cliffs, NJ: Messner, 1991.

Pedersen, Alwin. *Polar Animals.* New York: Taplinger Pub. Co., 1966.

Sandak, Cass R. *The Arctic and Antarctic.* New York: Franklin Watts, 1987.

Taylor, Barbara. *Arctic and Antarctic.* New York: Knopf, Distributed by Random House, 1995.